Business Presentation Strategies

Jonathan Li

Business Presentation Strategies

Copyright © 2014 by Jonathan Li

All rights reserved. No part of this book may be reproduced or transmitted in any form or by any means without written permission of the author.

Published by CreateSpace Independent Publishing Platform

Book Cover design by idrewdesign

Editing and Formatting by Jennifer Hampton

About The Author

Jonathan Li is the founder of ExpressiveDegrees.com who helps executives influence people and get what they want through leadership and business presentation online courses, monthly group coaching and online community.

As an effective business presentation coach, he has presented to different institutes and corporates. Over 11,000 executives rely on his advice for creating and delivering business presentations effectively.

Jonathan believes that every executive can create and deliver effective business presentations. With that focus, he's been involved with business presentations and has coached thousands of students to Business Presentation success.

About This Book
Imagine this: your audience gave you a standing ovation, your client was smiling and handing you a signed contract, your supervisor came to you and said, "Thank you! We're so glad to have you."

The world has changed.

You can influence people and get what you want by making effective business presentations. Mastering business presentations lets you eliminate whatever's blocking you and take back control of your future, instead of leaving your future in someone else's hands.

Business presentations make it all possible - and I know your message is worth sharing.

My history with Business Presentations is a long one. I used to struggle to express ideas effectively.

When my audience receives my message through business presentations, everything changes. Business Presentations have helped me influence more people than I could have ever imagined; with less time and effort than I could have dreamed; for more money than I would have guessed.

It's been an exciting journey.

I love Business Presentations and it is a big part of my career. I have delivered dozens of business presentations (for myself and others), taught courses to thousands of students and created online coaching programs on the topic.

So, about this book…

Over the years, I get asked many of the same questions over and over. Questions such as…

- What is a business presentation?
- Why is business presentation important?
- How do I make a business presentation?

- How do I start a business presentation?
- How to handle tough questions during a business presentation?
- And more…

In this book I answer those questions and 13 others. You will discover how to create and deliver business presentations effectively and persuasively.

When done, you should be able to take this valuable information and plot your own Business Presentation Strategies (just like the title).

This book is part of a large project for Mastering Influence and other coaching programs, of which I am the Creator. If you want to take your business presentation skills to the next level, I recommend you to check these practical resources.

There may be typos in this book and that we missed a few things. Do me a favor to sign up for our free training (instructions a few pages back) so we can keep you up to date as things change.

Express your dreams,
Jonathan Li
Hong Kong
Business Presentation Strategies
February 2014

Table of Contents

1. What is A Business Presentation? 1

2. Why Is Business Presentation Important?...............................2

3. What are the Top 3 Business Presentation Mistakes Most Executives Make? 3

4. How can I Make a Business Presentation? 6

5. How do I Start A Business Presentation?..................................9

6. What are the Ways to End a Business Presentation? 11

7. What are the Basic Rules of Business Presentation?.............13

8. What are the Effective Methods for Rehearsing a Business Presentation?..15

9. How can I Make My Business Presentations More Persuasive? 17

10. Does Practice Make Perfect? 19

11. How do You Handle Tough Questions During a Business Presentation? 21

12. How Many Slides should I Use in My Business Presentation? 24

13. What Business Presentation Software should I Use?...........26

14. What is the Role of Humor in Business Presentation? 28

15. How can I Gather Information for My Business Presentations?..30

16. How can I Come Up with a Catchy Title for a Business Presentation?" 32

17. How can I Look More Professional in a Business Presentation? 34

18. How can I Make My Business Presentations More Powerful? 36

19. What's My Next Step?......................................38

Sign Up for Our Free Training..................................39

Notes..41

1. What is A Business Presentation?

We need to give business presentations in many situations. It can be a sales meeting, a meeting with your clients, or even a business presentation with a big group of people. So basically when you need to deliver a message about business and it's more than two people, this is already a business presentation. That means your business presentation skills determine your career success. The better your business presentation skills, the higher chance you're going to become successful as a business person.

Summary:

When you deliver a business-related message to more than 2 people, you are already giving a business presentation.

Your Action Steps:

- Accept that you are giving business presentations regularly.
- Practice your business presentation skills whenever you have an opportunity.

2. Why Is Business Presentation Important?

There are many benefits of being an effective business presenter. Here are just a few of them:

- You will move ahead of our competitors and be on top of your industry.
- You will persuade other people to agree with what you are saying or doing.
- You will increase sales and maximize returns.
- You will gain respect of other people.
- You will break free from being tongue-tied when you are put on the spot with your clients and co-workers.
- You will get promoted faster and earn more money.

Summary:

Being an effective business presenter allows you to influence people and get what you want.

Your Action Steps:

- Start improving your business presentation skills today by applying the strategies in this book.
- Take a course or seminar on how to create and deliver business presentations effectively and persuasively.

3. What are the Top 3 Business Presentation Mistakes Most Executives Make?

Mistake #1: They give a boring opening.

Have you ever seen executives giving a business presentation, and they say something like, "Good morning everyone! My name is Jonathan LI, and today the topic I am going to talk about is, blah, blah, blah…"

How do you feel? It's so boring! Instead of making your audience feel bored, start with a BANG.

You can either ask a question, or start with a story. This could help you immediately grab the audience's attention and make them pay attention to you throughout the whole presentation.

Mistake #2: They end with the Q&A.

Do you know when does the audience remember your points the best? The opening… and also the closing, exactly! To make people remember your closing the best, repeat your key message and suggest their next steps.

Instead of answering questions from the audience, repeat your key message at the end of your presentation. You will then make sure the audience remember what you say and take action. If you want to have Q&A, fine; put it before the conclusion. You can first answer people's questions and then close strong. This is a win-win situation for both you and the audience.

Mistake #3: They only use logic.

Have you ever just heard a business presenter saying, "This proposal is perfect for your company because of reason one, reason two, reason three…?" This method is not effective. After all, we human beings are not just moved by logic, we are also moved by emotions.

When the speaker engages us with emotions, we feel, "Oh, this proposal works for me." And then we to use logic (or reasons) to justify our emotions. For example, when you are emotionally connected to an Apple ad, you say, "Oh, here's the newest Apple product. I love it! I want to buy it!" And then you just come up with reasons. "My iPad is old. Gotta buy a new one." "I heard this new version has higher quality. It's lighter. It's thinner." And then what did you do? You line up and buy this newest Apple product!

Emotions are powerful. Engage your audience with emotions through storytelling, and you will get more clients and boost your sales.

3. What are the Top 3 Business Presentation Mistakes Most Executives Make?

Summary:

- Open your business presentation with a question or story.
- Do the Q&A before your closing.
- Engage your audience with emotions so they will become your loyal clients.

Your Action Steps:

- Open your next business presentation with a question or story.
- Close your next business presentation by repeating your key message and suggesting clear next steps.
- Emotionally engage with your audience through storytelling.

4. How can I Make a Business Presentation?

There is a proven process to make an effective and persuasive business presentation. I applied this process to outspeak 3,000 contestants and became one of the winners in the Hong Kong Public Speaking Competition. People pay me thousands of dollars just to learn this proven method. Right now, I am going to show you exactly how you can make effective business presentations.

Introducing... The Web Model.

Step 1: Create your Power Phrase.

What's a Power Phrase? A Power Phrase is your message. It determines what should be included or excluded from your speech. Remember, your message should be no more than 12 words because this makes your presentation a lot more memorable.

One of my most famous keynote presentations is called, "Influence People And Get What You Want: Effective Executive Presentations." My Power Phrase in this presentation is, "Every business executive can express their ideas effectively." That's my Power Phrase. I then focus on finding information that support my key message so people believe in my message and take action. I challenge you to do the same.

Step 2: Use stories.

Bill Gove, the first President of National Speaker's Association once said, "Public speaking is very simple. Just tell a story and make a point. Tell another story, make another point." To prove your point, think about what stories you can tell. These stories doesn't need to be the bedtime stories you listened to when you were a kid. It can be your personal experience, or a case study from your clients, or even the news you just have read today. All these stories can be supporting materials that make your presentation more persuasive.

Step 3: Write your opening and closing.

Your audience remembers your opening and closing the best. Since these 2 parts are so important, I have written two specific chapters on creating a attention-grabbing opening and memorable closing. See you in the next chapter.

Summary:

The Web Model makes your business presentations more effective and persuasive.

Your Action Steps:
- Make your business presentations with this Web Model.
- Create your Power Phrase
- Use stories to support your point(s).

- Write your opening and closing.

5. How do I Start A Business Presentation?

You only have 7 seconds to grab the audience's attention. That's why you need to start with a BANG. Here are 2 powerful ways for you to use immediately:

1. Ask a You-focused question

Have you…? Would you…? Could you…? There's always a "you" in the question. The more you use "you", the more the audience feels that you are talking directly to them. They will pay close attention to your presentation and of course your message. For example, you can start a business presentation by saying "Would you like to influence people and get what you want?"

Simple question, powerful results.

2. Start with a story

Human beings are moved by emotions and logic. We can easily combine both elements with a story. If I give a business presentation on customer service, I would start with, "If you were sitting next to me on the black leather sofa in the living room 5 years ago, you would have seen me waiting for the customer service manager impatiently…"

Immediately, the audience will be drawn to your story, and you get their attention in less than 7 seconds.

Summary:

To grab your audience's attention in 7 seconds, start with a You-focused question or a story.

Your Action Steps:

- Start your next business presentation with either a You-focused question or a story.
- Write out your opening so you know exactly what to say.
- Practice your opening in front of a friend or colleague until you can deliver it confidently.

6. What are the Ways to End a Business Presentation?

There are 3 ways to make your business presentation ending more memorable.

1. Summarize your key points

At the end of your presentation, make sure the audience remembers what you say. One effective way is to do a quick summary. You can say, "Alright, today we've gone through 3 important points. They are Point #1... Point #2... Point #3..." Clear and simple.

2. Repeat your Power Phrase.

At the end of my keynote presentation, I may repeat my Power Phrase, "Remember, every business executive can express their ideas effectively," Now your audience locks your key message in their mind.

3. Suggest next steps.

Make sure you show what next step your audience should take. The next step could be investing in your company or signing the insurance contract. When you provide people with clear next steps, they are going to take action immediately.

Summary:

End your business presentations with a short summary, Power Phrase and clear next steps.

Your Action Steps:

- Write a short summary based on your points.
- Repeat your Power Phrase.
- At the end of your presentation, suggest clear next steps.

7. What are the Basic Rules of Business Presentation?

Here are some important basic rules that you must remember.

Rule #1: Your business presentation must be conversational.

The world has changed. It's no longer about using business jargons to show how professional you are, how great you are, how experience you are. In the new world, we focus on being conversational. Just like you are having conversations with your friends in the living room.

The more friendly and relaxed you are, the better you can connect with the audience. This is how you can make effective business presentations. So keep your language simple and conversational.

Rule #2: Make sure your presentation is You-focused.

A lot of people introduce their products or company by saying, "Our company is the # 1 expert in this field. We have so many clients and blah, blah, blah, blah, blah," Your clients and the audience just don't care. What your audience focus on is, "What's in it for me?"

You should therefore focus on the benefits you can bring to your clients. For instance," Our services will help you achieve financial freedom so you don't have worry about paying your bills anymore." When you make your presentation You-focused, you build an instant connection with the audience. Now they feel that you care about them, and they will be more likely to take your advice.

Summary:

The two basics rules of business presentations are being conversational and You-focused.

Your Action Steps:

- Remove all unnecessary jargons in your presentations. Make sure your language is simple and easy-to-understand.
- Review your business presentation and ask yourself, "How can I make my presentation more You-focused?"
- List out the benefits your products and services can bring to your clients. Make sure you mention the key benefits in your business presentations.

8. What are the Effective Methods for Rehearsing a Business Presentation?

One of the biggest rehearsal mistakes I have seen people make is that they try to practice in front of a mirror. This is just not effective. Picture that, when you are looking in front of a mirror, you may think, "Oh, my hair looks terrible. Gotta fix my hair." "Oh, I need to change my shirt." "I look so tired." See? You are focusing on yourself, not your audience.

The most effective rehearsing method is to record and review your business presentation. Do you have a smartphone or maybe a webcam? Great! Because that's all you need. Here's what I want you to do. Take out your smartphone, your iPhone or anything with recording functions, and record your presentation rehearsal. Later on you can sit down and relax, maybe grab some popcorn, and review your presentation. Now you are watching the rehearsal from the audience's perspective, and you are going to know how to improve.

Reviewing the rehearsal video, you may feel that, "Oh, I need more eye contact." Now you can write that down, "More eye contact." And you can work on that next time. That is how you can improve your public speaking skills quickly and create effective business presentations.

Another effective method is to rehearse your presentation in Toastmasters. Toastmasters is an international organization that helps you improve your communication skills effectively. Take a 5-7 minute segment of your presentation and deliver it in front of the Toastmasters audience. You will receive direct feedback from a live audience. This first-hand feedback can help you improve your business presentation, influence more people and get what you want.

Summary:

Rehearse your business presentation in front of a video camera or live audience.

Your Action Steps:

- Record your next business presentation in front of a video-recording device.
- Review the video and ask yourself, "How can I make this presentation even better?"
- Rehearse your speech at a local Toastmasters club. Get direct feedback from a live audience.

9. How can I Make My Business Presentations More Persuasive?

Yes, your business presentation needs to be persuasive. If you don't persuade, how can you affect and motivate the audience to take action? Here's one thing you must do to make your presentation more persuasive: Use stories.

Stories are very, very powerful and persuasive because it combines both emotions and logic. When you use these two elements at the same time, you'll create massive value for your audience. They just feel that, "Oh, yes, exactly! I should do this!" What you can do is to share your personal experiences. Let's say you are selling insurance to prospects. You may say, "Last year, my friend David got Pancreas cancer. Because he didn't buy insurance, he couldn't afford to stay in the top hospital and receive the best treatment. He passed away 2 months later…"

Immediately, your prospects feel that, "Oh, if I don't buy insurance, I am going to be in big trouble just like his friend. I may die. I don't wanna die!" See? The prospects start to use logic to justify their emotions. "Right, $2,000 a month isn't that expensive. I can handle that." And then they sign the contract and become your newest clients.

Want to make your presentation more persuasive? Remember to use stories.

Summary:

Stories are the lifeblood to make your business presentations more persuasive.

Your Action Steps:

- Reflect on your personal experiences. Think about what stories you can use to support the key points in your next business presentation.
- Open a folder and save your personal stories that can be potential proof for your business presentations. This will save you tons of time when making presentations.

Chapter 10

10. Does Practice Make Perfect?

When we were at school, we were taught, "Practice makes perfect." Unfortunately, this is not true. In fact, practice doesn't make perfect, practice with evaluation makes great improvement.

How can you get quality evaluation from people? One of the most powerful ways is to get coaching.

When I got promoted the Hong Kong Public Speaking Competition final, I was doing well. But I knew that if I wanted to succeed and give a powerful business presentation, I would need coaching. I needed to get feedback from the best people around me. So I went to my mentor, Bill. He's a 30-year-old senior lecturer who has native European English accent. I said, "Bill, I know you have created more winners in this competition than anyone else. I know you are the best. Can you coach me so I can win this competition too?" Bill looked me in the eyes and said, "Yes, Jonathan."

Every week we met up, and I gave my 5-minute presentation. And Bill coached me on how to improve my presentation skills. He would say "Jonathan, your eye contact's not good enough; make sure you look at the audience in a much friendlier way so you can build a better connection with them." "Jonathan, use better pronunciation. It should be limelight in the darrrk." I listened to him and I did not question him. By applying these strategies, I outspoke 3,000 contestants and became one of the winners. That's the power of coaching.

When you get coaching, you're going to improve public speaking skills more quickly, and become a more persuasive speaker. Get coaching.

Summary:

Practice doesn't make perfect; practice with evaluation makes great improvement.

Your Action Steps:

- Practice and get quality feedback from a person who is more experienced and capable in business presentations.
- Find a coach that can help you improve business presentation skills quickly.
- Ask for advice from the best speaker in your organization. Ask, "How can I make my business presentation more effective?"

Chapter 11

11. How do You Handle Tough Questions During a Business Presentation?

When you give a business presentation, it's common to get questions from your audience. This audience member can be your supervisor, your client, or even your subordinates. The audience will always ask you questions. So, when you get a tough question, what should you do?

The best thing for you to do is to prepare beforehand. To predict the questions you may get, you don't need a magic crystal ball. All you need is one thing - your common sense. If you're selling a public speaking product, you may predict the following possible questions:

- Why is public speaking so important?
- What are the steps we'll need to take in order to improve our public speaking skills quickly?
- Where can I find the best public speaking coach for me to achieve my business goals?

These may be the possible questions you get from the audience. I want you to write down the possible questions people may ask you in your next business presentation, and invest some time to practice. If you get this question, how are you going to answer it? As a result, when you really get this question in the Q&A, you can answer it very naturally and confidently.

"But what if I couldn't predict that question?" If you get a question that you don't have the answer, don't try to make it up. Be professional; look into the eyes of your audience and say, *"That's an interesting question, and now since it's a really thought-provoking question, I need some more time to give you the best answer, so how about this? Can I come back to you at 5 p.m. today? I will send you an email replying to your question."* In most cases, your audience are very reasonable, and they are going to agree.

With this technique, you remain professional, and answer your audience's question effectively.

Summary:

The best way to handle tough questions is to predict them beforehand.

Your Action Steps:

- Brainstorm the possible questions you will be asked in the next business presentation.
- Practice answering these questions so you will feel more confident and natural.

Chapter 11

- When you don't know how to answer a tough question, offer an alternative of answering this question in a moment.

12. How Many Slides should I Use in My Business Presentation?

The last question you should ask is how many slides you should use in a business presentation. After all, the first thing we need to do is to come up with a message.

Create your message first, and then think about whether you should use a slide or not. I have seen people who don't use slides, and they can still win their client's hearts and get a big contract; I have also seen people who use hundreds of slides in a 45 minute presentation, and they still perform very well. Both ways work. The key is to decide whether the slides support your message.

If your slides support your message, use it. If not, leave it out. After all, the people should focus on your message, not your slides.

Summary:

The question is not, "how many slides should I use in my business presentation?" The question should be, "Does this slide support my message?"

Your Action Steps:

- Create your key message before using a single presentation slide.

12. How Many Slides should I Use in My Business Presentation?

- Ask yourself, "Does this slide support my message?"
- If yes, keep the slide. If no, leave it out. It's that simple.

13. What Business Presentation Software should I Use?

There are lots of shiny business presentation softwares nowadays. Most people use Microsoft PowerPoint for their presentations. I don't think this will make you stand out as a presenter. If you really want to stand out as a business presenter, there are more professional softwares that you can consider.

You can use this amazing Apple software called Keynote. It's very easy-to-use. Simply choose a blank background, use powerful visuals with minimum words. You've got a powerful business presentation! This is so far one of the most effective softwares for you to make presentation slides.

If your presentation is more creative and brainstorming-related, you can consider using Prezi. Prezi is a very powerful animation software which allows your presentation to move around. This provides your audience with an exciting visual experience, making your presentation more engaging.

Make sure you find the presentation software is easy to use, and you can control it. Then you can use this software to create effective and powerful business presentations.

13. What Business Presentation Software should I Use?

Summary:

PowerPoint is losing its power. To stand out from your competitors, use Apple Keynote or Prezi.

Your Action Steps:

- Check out the amazing Apple Keynote software and Prezi this week.
- Decide which presentation software you find is more easy-to-use.
- Use this software to create your next business presentation that requires slides (or visual aids.)

14. What is the Role of Humor in Business Presentation?

The person who asked this question is already smart, really smart. You know why? Because a lot of people when they try to give a business presentation, they think that, "I shouldn't use humor. I need to be serious because humour makes make me unprofessional."

The role of humor is about connecting with your audience. Picture that… Your clients listen to presentations almost every day. So what would they feel if they know they have to listen to another presentation again? "Ahhhhh, another business presentation, and it's going to be so boring!" If you make the audience feel good and relaxed by injecting humour in your business presentations, they will pay more attention and act on your advice.

Humor is not about telling cheap jokes: the jokes you see online, on a talk show or a comedy. The best source of humour is organic. What is organic humor? Organic humor is about the humor you uncover from your stories. It can be a failure you have recently faced or a funny experience that supports your message. Sharing your personal experiences in presentations helps you relate to the audience. With a common experience, you can immediately make the audience laugh. When your audience laugh, they are going to pay attention to your business presentations.

Chapter 14

Uncover humor in your business presentations, and you are going to make your audience laugh and make a big impact.

Summary:

The role of humor is all about connecting with your audience; and the best source of humor is organic.

Your Action Steps:

- Find the common ground between you and your audience.
- Recall what personal experiences you can use to support your point(s).
- Be willing to laugh at yourself. It lightens up your presentations and make the audience pay more attention to your message.

15. How can I Gather Information for My Business Presentations?

We are so lucky! In the past, when we need to gather information, we had to go to the library and check out piles of old newspapers. Nowadays, we can just go online and search tons of information.

To gather firsthand information for your business presentations, interview your audience beforehand. Before I deliver a business presentation, I usually ask my key contact or key client, "Can you give me 5 names from the audience that I can interview before my presentation?" I will also get their email address or phone number, and I will ask these people 2 very important questions. Hope you'll do the same because this can make a big impact in your career.

Question 1: What frustrates you right now?

When you know the frustrations your audience are facing, you can build up the pain and relate to them easily. "Yeah, I can't sleep well at night because I am always worried about my job security and financial future." When you build up the pain, the audience will feel that, "Wow, this presenter knows me so well! I am going to pay attention to him, and let's see what he's gonna say."

Chapter 15

Question 2: What challenges are you facing right now?

People pay top experts to solve their problems. When you understand your client's challenges, and customize your presentation to solve their challenges, you will be admired as the ultimate expert in your field. You gain their trust. When you gain trust, you can do business with people more easily.

Next time when you give a business presentation, remember to do research on your audience and ask them these two questions. Then you can customize a business presentation that is more specific and powerful.

Summary:

To gather firsthand information for your business presentations, interview your audience beforehand.

Your Action Steps:

- Ask your key contact for 5 names so you can interview them before your business presentation.
- Ask these people the 2 questions, "What frustrates you right now?" "What challenges are you facing right now?"
- Use these helpful answers to relate to your corporate audience during your presentations.

16. How can I Come Up with a Catchy Title for a Business Presentation?"

Yeah, right! A catchy title makes your audience curious about, "What is this presenter going to say? This is interesting!" They stop checking their smartphone; they stop checking their email; and they *start* focusing on your presentation. So how can you come up with a catchy title?

1. Make sure your title is benefit-driven.

Your title is the first subject that your audience sees. Make sure that the audience members know exactly what benefits they will get. My signature keynote presentation is called *"Influence People and Get What You Want: How to Make Effective Executive Presentations."* What benefits do you think the audience will get? Yes, "Influence people and get what you want."

Reading the title, your audience will learn the benefits and feel excited to hear your presentation. Congrats, you've got their attention!

2. Make your title YOU-focused.

We want to make sure that the audience know that the presentation is not about us. It's about the audience: your clients, your supervisor, your audience. Focus on "you"; put a "you" in the title.

16. How can I Come Up with a Catchy Title for a Business Presentation?"

Just like my title suggests, "Influence People And Get What *You* Want." These two simple techniques helps you build a deeper connection with the corporate audience.

Summary:

A catchy business presentation title is benefit-driven and you-focused.

Your Action Steps:

- Before coming up with a title, ask yourself, "What benefits will my audience get from my business presentation?"
- Make your title is YOU-focused.
- Ask your colleagues and friends whether they find your title catchy and interesting. If not, review the title and test again.

17. How can I Look More Professional in a Business Presentation?

Great business presenters are professional, always. No matter what happens, we need to remain professional. Here are 3 simple and effective techniques to look more professional in a business presentation.

1. Have someone introduce you before your presentation.

Telling people how great you are is pointless, especially when you are bragging. To let the audience know more about you, have someone introduce you before delivering a presentation. One easy way is to have the meeting planner or organizer read your introduction. Of course, you first need to write a short introduction that shows your credentials and the benefits your audience will get from your presentations. This small tweak can boost your credibility and make you look more professional.

2. Use a wireless presenter

Have you ever seen a business presenter moving back and forth, trying to click to the next slide with a mouse? This is so annoying and unprofessional. Take control of technology, or technology will take control of you. The solution is to get a wireless professional presenter. My favourite brand is Kensington. Their presenters are easy-to-use, with a laser pointer (which is very useful for drawing attention to important data.) You can easily

17. How can I Look More Professional in a Business Presentation?

get one at a computer store. Using a wireless presenter immediately positions you as a top professional.

3. "B" more

Too many presenters try to fight for attention between themselves and the screen. When the audience don't know what to focus on, they give up. Make sure you show the audience what to concentrate on. When you do the talking, you want to make the screen blank, so the audience members can focus on you. You can simply achieve this goal by clicking the "B" button on your wireless presenter. Yay! You've got another reason to buy a professional presenter.

Summary:

You need 2 tools to make yourself more professional: a speaker introduction and a wireless presenter.

Your Action Steps:

- Write a short speaker introduction by stating your credentials and the benefits your audience will get from the presentation.
- Buy a wireless presenter with a laser pointer.
- Practice using the "B" button in presentations so the audience will focus on you.

18. How can I Make My Business Presentations More Powerful?

When asking my clients, "Why do you want to make a good presentation?" They say, "I want to gain more power. I want to climb up the corporate ladder and become a more successful leader." Good news! You are in the right place at the right time. Making effective business presentations helps you gain more power than anything else. Your ability to express ideas effectively gives you a competitive edge.

So how can you make powerful presentations?

Come up with a Power Phrase. A Power Phrase is your message; the reason why it is so powerful is that the Power Phrase determines what should be included or excluded in your presentation. If a story, statistic, or activity supports your message, put it in your presentation. If it fails to support your point, leave it out.

When you are laser-focused on what to say, you're going to make business presentations more powerful, because the audience remembers your point even days or even weeks after your presentation. As a result, they will be more likely to agree with your points and do business with you. So the key to powerful presentation is to come up with a Power Phrase.

18. How can I Make My Business Presentations More Powerful?

Also make sure your Power Phrase has no more than 12 words so the message is more punchy and memorable. When the audience remembers what you say, you can influence people and get what you want; you gain more power.

Summary:

The key to powerful presentations is to come up with a Power Phrase; your message.

Your Action Steps:

- Create your Power Phrase by summarizing your business presentation in 1 simple sentence.
- Shorten your Power Phrase to no more than 12 words.
- Find stories, statistics or case studies to support your Power Phrase.

19. What's My Next Step?

All right! We've gone through the top 18 questions on business presentations. Now you have the strategies on your hand to make effective and persuasive business presentations.

I am frequently asked, "Jonathan, I love your ideas. What's my next step?" Go to my website, ExpressiveDegrees.com and sign up for my free video training. You are going to receive more practical tools on how to create and deliver effective business presentations so you will influence people and get what you want.

So, go out there, give your business presentation and make an impact today.

Sign Up for Our Free Training

The word of Business Presentation is changing all the time. We want to make sure you are kept up to date with the latest information.

We also have a few resources (that can't fit into a traditional book) that we'd like to send you.

This is simply a way for us to offer you more value.

Sign up for our free training so we can keep you up to date with all things about Business Presentation. Other than updates, we'd like to send you the following resources, that couldn't, obviously, be included here:

- A video training series on how to influence people and get what you want by creating and delivering effective business presentations.

- The 5 proven steps I use everyday to make persuasive business presentations (Hint: Executives literally beg me to take their money)

- Access to our online community (with top executives all around the world)

- A few more bonuses that we want to surprise you with.

- To sign up for free training, go now to:

http://ExpressiveDegrees.com

Notes

Berkun, Scott. *Confessions of A Public Speaker*. California: O'Reilly, 2010. Print.

Brown, Mark, et al., *Speaker's EDGE: Secrets and Strategies for Connecting with Any Audience*. Arkansas: Soar, 2010. Print.

Carnegie, Dale. *Public Speaking for Success*. New York: Penguin, 2005. Print.

Carnegie, Dale. *The Quick & Easy Way to Effective Speaking*. New York: Pocket, 1962. Print.

Donovan, Jeremey. *How to Deliver A TED Talk: Secrets of the World's Most Inspiring Presentations*. Columbus: McGraw-Hill, 2014. Print.

Gallo, Carmine. *The Presentation Secrets of Steve Jobs: How to Be Insanely Great in Front of Any Audience*. New York: McGraw-Hill, 2010. Print.

Karia, Akash. *How to Deliver the Perfect TED Talk: Presentation Secrets of the World's Best Speakers*, 2013. Web. 21 Nov. 2013.

Kushner, Malcolm. *Presentations for Dummies*. New Jersey: Wiley, 2004. Print.

Marshall, Lisa B. Smart Talk: How to Make Genuine Conversations, Build Lasting Relationships and Influence Others. New York, 2013. Griffin, 2013. Web. 4 Jan. 2013.

Maxwell, John C. *Everyone Communicates, Few Connect: What the Most Effective People Do Differently*. Nashville: Thomas Nelson, 2010. Print.

Miller, Anne. *Metaphorically Selling: How to Use the Magic of Metaphors to Sell, Persuade, & Explain Anything to Anyone.* New York: Chiron, 2004. Print.

Monarth, Harrison, and Larina Kase. *The Confident Speaker: Beat Your Nerves and Communicate at Your Best in Any Situation.* New York: McGraw-Hill, 2007. Print.

Reynolds, Garr. *Presentation Zen Design: Simple Design Principles and Techniques to Enhance Your Presentations.* Berkeley: New Riders, 2010. Print.

Reynolds, Garr. *Presentation Zen: Simple Ideas on Presentation Design and Delivery.* Berkeley: New Riders, 2012. Print.

Tracy, Brian. *Speak to Win: How to Present with Power in Any Situation.* New York: AMACOM, 2008. Print.

Valentine, Craig, and Mitch Meyerson. *World Class Speaking: The Ultimate Guide to Presenting, Marketing and Profiting like a Champion.* New York: Morgan, 2009. Print.

Walker, TJ. *How to Give A Pretty Good Presentation.* New Jersey: Wiley, 2010. Print.

Weiss, Alan. *Money Talks: How to Make A Million As A Speaker.* New York: McGraw-Hill, 1998. Print.

Weissman, Jerry. *In The Line of Fire: How to Handle Tough Questions… When It Counts.* New Jersey: Pearson, 2005. Print.

Weissman, Jerry. *Presenting to Win: The Art of Telling Your Story.* New Jersey: Pearson, 2009. Print.

www.ingramcontent.com/pod-product-compliance
Lightning Source LLC
Chambersburg PA
CBHW071825170526
45167CB00003B/1419